FOOD FOR EVERYONE

Brenda Walpole

W

FRANKLIN WATTS
LONDON·SYDNEY

First published in 2008 by
Franklin Watts
338 Euston Road, London NW1 3BH

Franklin Watts Australia
Level 17/207 Kent Street, Sydney, NSW 2000

EARTH SOS is based on the series *Earth Watch* published by Franklin Watts. It
was produced for Franklin Watts by Bender Richardson White, P O Box 266,
Uxbridge UB9 5NX.
Project Editor: Lionel Bender
Text Editor: Jenny Vaughan
Original text adapted and updated by: Jenny Vaughan
Designer: Ben White
Picture Researchers: Cathy Stastny and Daniela Marceddu
Media Conversion and Make-up: Mike Weintroub, MW Graphics,
and Clare Oliver
Production: Kim Richardson

For Franklin Watts:
Series Editor: Melanie Palmer
Art Director: Jonathan Hair
Cover design: Chi Leung

A CIP catalogue record for this book is available from the British Library.

ISBN 978 0 7496 7675 9

Dewey classification 338.1'9

Printed in China

Picture Credits: Oxford Scientific Films: cover main photo (Ronald Toms)
and pages 11 top (Paul McCullagh), 12-13 (Raymond Blythe), 29 top (Raj
Sing). Bruce Coleman Ltd.: cover small photo (Jens Rydell). Ecoscene: pages
1 & 24 (Sally Morgan), 5 top (Mike Maidment), 8 left (Tim Page), 15
bottom right (Ken Ayres). Panos Pictures: pages 8-9 (Neil Cooper), 14
(Allison Wright), 27 bottom (Betty Press). Environmental Images: pages 7
bottom (Venessa Miles), 21 bottom left (Chris Martin). Science Photo Library,
London: pages 12 (Debra Ferguson), 17 bottom left (Peter Menzel), 18
(Tomasso Guiccicardini), 19 top (Cape Grim BAPS/Simon Fraser), 19 bottom
(NASA), 22 and 23 (Ed Young/Agstock). Tony Stone Images: pages 6 and 16
(Andy Sacks), 21 top right (James Strachan), 25 top (Vito Palmisano), 25
bottom (Chuck Keeler). Corbis Images: pages 4 (Philip Gould), 17 top right
(Hans Georg Roth), 26 (Gary Braasch), 28 (George Lepp). Still Pictures:
pages 5 bottom (Carlos Guarita), 7 top and 13 (Jorgen Schytte), 11 bottom
and 27 top (Mark Edwards), 15 top left (Peter Frischmuth). Cafédirect: page
29 bottom.

Artwork by Raymond Turvey

Franklin Watts is a division of Hachette Children's Books, an Hachette Livre
UK company.

Note to parents and teachers:
Every effort has been made by the
publisher to ensure that websites
listed are suitable for children, that
they are of the highest educational
value, and that they contain no
inappropriate or offensive material.
However, because of the nature of
the Internet, it is impossible to
guarantee that the contents of
these sites will not be altered. We
strongly advise that Internet access
is supervised by a responsible adult.

CONTENTS

FEEDING THE WORLD

There are twice as many people on Earth as there were 50 years ago. We are growing a lot more food than we used to. But many people still do not get enough to eat.

More from the land

There are more than six billion people on Earth. To feed everyone, we will have to grow more food than we have ever done before. One way to do this is by using more land for farms. But not all land is good for farming. Also, if we clear land to make farms, it can harm the environment.

In some countries, farms produce more food than they need. It has to be stored until it is sold.

Machines help farmers produce more food. These are mechanical milking machines.

New technology

New machines and new ways of farming can help us get more food from the land. There are new kinds of wheat, fruit and vegetables, which grow faster than old ones. New breeds of animals give us more meat or more milk.

Food supply

In some countries, farmers grow more food than the people need. They sell food to other countries. But some countries are too poor to buy food or cannot grow enough themselves. Many people may go hungry.

*When there is a **drought** or a war, people may not be able to grow enough food. This is a camp in Africa. Food is given to people in need.*

Eco Thought
Around 240,000 babies are born each day, and many will live much longer than in the past.

FARMING TODAY

There are many different kinds of farms. Some are huge, modern farms with a lot of machines. Others are much smaller.

Small farms

All over the world, there are small farms that are run by just one family. Some are **subsistence farms.** Here, the farmers may grow crops only for themselves and their children, and keep a few animals for milk and meat. Many small farms also grow food to sell. Some farms are **organic farms.** On these farms the farmers grow crops without using chemicals such as **pesticides** or **fertilizers.**

On small farms, most of the work is done by hand.

A small farm in India. Cattle are used to pull the ploughs.

Larger farms

On large farms, nearly everything that is grown is sold. There may be big fields of cereals, with sprinklers to water them. Farmers use machines to plough the fields, sow the seeds and harvest the grain. These farms do not need many workers. This is called **intensive farming**. Farming this way means ten times more food will grow on a piece of land than using old-fashioned methods.

This machine is cutting maize. It separates the grain and puts it into a truck.

Ranches

Ranches are the biggest farms of all. They are grassland farms for cattle (cows). Most ranches are in North and South America and Australia.

STAPLE CROPS

There are important foods our bodies need to give us energy. We call these staple foods. They can be cereals, such as rice; or roots, such as potatoes. We call the land they grow on arable land.

Rice plants are planted by hand in muddy fields.

Vital foods

Staple crops contain a lot of starch, which give us energy. In cooler countries, staple crops include potatoes, wheat and barley. In hot countries, they include maize (sweetcorn) and rice. Often, grains are used to make flour for bread, biscuits or pasta.

Harvesting potatoes. The first potatoes came from South America, but they now grow all over the world.

Rice as a staple food

More than half the people in the world eat rice every day. Rice grows in hot countries. Most rice grows best in very wet fields called paddies. These are mainly in tropical parts of Asia. However, there are some kinds that will grow in drier places.

Eco Thought

In the United States, each person eats around 3,500 **calories** a day. Less than half of these calories come from staple foods. People in Central Africa eat half as much, but nearly all are staple foods.

Crops for cash

In many countries around the world, farmers grow crops to sell. These include tea and coffee, or tobacco. We call these **cash crops.** The farmers can use the money to buy food. But many people think it is better if the farmers grow their own food.

Try this

Work out how many staple foods you eat. Include cereals, root crops, and peas, beans and lentils.

There is over 738,000 square kilometres of farmland in Canada. It is mostly used for cereals.

CARING FOR SOIL

Plants take in water through their roots. They also take in nutrients (substances that help them grow). Farmers can make the soil better by adding nutrients to it.

Nutrient cycles

When wild plants die, they rot. **Nutrients** in them go back into the soil. When crops are harvested, there are no rotting plants, so farmers must add new nutrients instead.

Adding nutrients

Farmers often add fertilizer to the soil, or they may plant turnips and let them rot in the ground. Often, they plant clover. All these are ways to add nutrients to the soil.

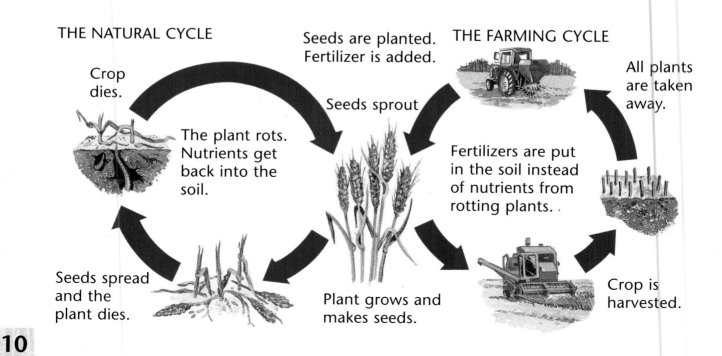

THE NATURAL CYCLE

Crop dies.

The plant rots. Nutrients get back into the soil.

Seeds spread and the plant dies.

Seeds are planted. Fertilizer is added.

Seeds sprout

Plant grows and makes seeds.

THE FARMING CYCLE

All plants are taken away.

Fertilizers are put in the soil instead of nutrients from rotting plants.

Crop is harvested.

Fertilizers

Manure (animal waste) and **compost** made from rotted plants are very good fertilizers. Artificial fertilizers are chemicals made in factories. These soak into the ground and help crops grow.

Manure is very good fertilizer for farmland.

Water

In dry places, farmers **irrigate** their land. Sometimes, they dig ditches so water can flow between the rows of plants. Some farmers have pumps and sprays to spread water over fields. Very dry soil can blow away, or be washed away by heavy rain.

Bad farming can harm the land. For example, too much water or fertilizer may have killed these trees.

PESTS

Pests damage one-fifth of all the crops we grow. Insects, slugs and weeds can destroy whole fields of crops. Farmers try to find ways of getting rid of pests, so they can save their crops.

Using pesticides

The chemicals that kill weeds and creatures that attack crops are called pesticides. Farmers spray pesticides on their crops. Pesticides that kill insects are called **insecticides.** The best ones are expensive. They kill harmful insects, but they do not hurt useful insects, such as bees. In poorer countries, farmers often have to use cheaper pesticides, which are more harmful to the environment.

This aircraft is spraying insecticide over a field.

Tiny insects called aphids damage crops. Ladybirds are useful to farmers, because they eat aphids.

On the Ground

In Indonesia, there was a problem with insects called leaf-hoppers. Other insects get rid of them better than insecticides can.

Scientists try to find a kind of rice that pests will not attack.

Eco Thought

Out of a million kinds of insects, about 4,000 harm crops or animals.

Natural pest control

A lot of people think too many chemical pesticides are bad for the environment. They say natural pesticides are better. Some farmers plant marigolds or onions with their crops. Many insects keep away from these because of their smell. There are also insects that attack pests. We call these natural predators. Farmers can also use special scents called **pheromones**. Insects will fly towards these, away from the crops.

LIVESTOCK

Farmers keep animals such as cattle (cows), pigs, sheep and goats. We call these livestock. They give us meat, milk, wool or leather. Farmers keep different livestock on different kinds of land.

Many people in Asia keep buffaloes. They are used as working animals, and for their milk.

Grazing animals

Farmers often keep livestock in fields as they eat grass. Cattle are kept in big groups called herds. They need very good grass. Groups of sheep are called flocks. Sheep can live in places where the grass is not good, and on steep hillsides. Farmers keep some cattle for their meat and others for milk. They keep sheep for meat and wool.

Eco Thought
There are over 1,000 million cattle in the world. There are about 300 million cows in India — one for every three people.

There are thousands of chickens in this shed. This is one example of factory farming.

Factory farms

On some farms, a lot of animals are kept together, indoors. They are given special food, to make them grow fast. We call this factory farming. It is a way to get meat quickly and cheaply. Pigs and chickens are often kept like this. Many people think it is cruel to keep animals this way. It is better to keep **free-range** animals, which live in larger spaces.

Try this
Which tastes better – free-range or factory-farmed meat and eggs?

The cost of freedom

Free-range animals can go outside during the day and move about. Many people think these animals are happier than ones on factory farms. But it is a more expensive way to keep animals.

These free-range pigs live outdoors most of the time. They have shelters called arks to go into in bad weather.

15

MORE FOOD

People first began farming about 10,000 years ago. They found wild plants and animals that they could use for food, and kept them on farms.

Better breeds

Scientists and farmers can make new types of plants and animals. They choose the best plants and animals and make new ones from these. Over many years, they end up with stronger, bigger plants and animals, or ones that give more food. Or they can breed plants and animals that live in different climates, or are easier to keep. All this is called selective breeding.

These cows are going to be given sperm from a bull the farmer has specially chosen.

Eco Thought

Most cows make about 5,000 litres of milk a year. But there are some that can make 16,000 litres a year.

New ideas

Farmers in Africa used to grow maize (sweetcorn). But now they are growing millet and sorghum grains instead. These grow better in hot, dry climates. In Asia and Australia, some farmers keep crocodiles and in South Africa, they keep ostriches. These animals provide meat and leather.

Ostriches are kept on farms in Africa, Europe, America and Australia.

On the Ground

Scientists have created a maize that is not harmed by weedkiller. But this may be bad for the environment.

Genetic engineering

Genes are tiny parts of living things. They are what make living things develop in certain ways. Scientists have learned to take genes from one kind of living thing, and put it into another. This is called **genetic engineering.** This can make living things that are able to resist pests, for example.

Scientists have used genetic engineering to make new kinds of maize (sweetcorn).

17

NEW TECHNOLOGY

Farmers today use modern technology. They use computers to keep records and to find out accurate weather forecasts.

These scientists are studying sorghum. They record what they find out on a computer.

Computer farmers

Farmers today use computers on their farms. They use them to work out things like how much fertilizer they need and which crops to grow. Knowing this can help them decide what sort of food to give to their livestock.

Weather forecasting

Satellites and weather stations help give farmers accurate weather forecasts. They need these to plan ahead. For example, they need to make sure they harvest crops when the weather is dry.

On the Ground

Weather satellites and computers help us know what the weather will be like weeks in advance.

This is a climate research station. It gives weather scientists useful information.

This photograph shows how much heat different things give off. Hedges show up as yellow. Fields of crops show up as red. The river is nearly black.

Bird's-eye view

Photographs taken from satellites show how the ground below reflects sunlight. The crops in the fields all show up as different colours. The pictures help scientists know which crops are growing well, and which ones are not.

FARMING THE SEAS

People have always caught fish. Now, new ways of fishing mean that too many fish are caught.

Fishing at sea

A lot of fishing is done in traditional ways. Small fishing boats pull nets called trawl nets along behind them. They stay at sea for a few days, and then go home to unload the fish. Now there are also big factory ships with even bigger nets. These can catch 100 tonnes of fish. They stay at sea for months.

Drift and trawl nets catch huge numbers of fish - but they may catch other animals, such as dolphins, too. Purse nets form a circle to catch thousands of fish.

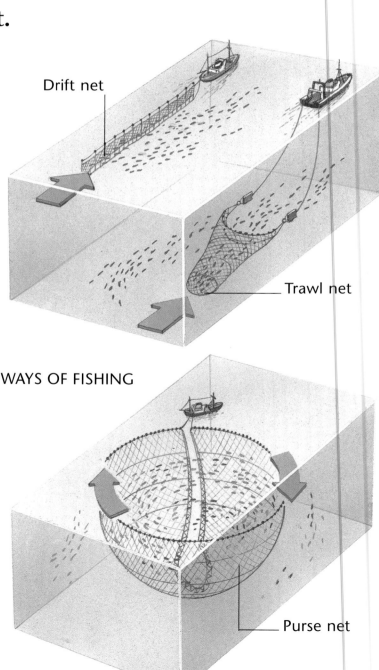

Drift net

Trawl net

WAYS OF FISHING

Purse net

Saving small fish

Factory ships catch more fish than the old boats. Their nets catch even the tiny fish so there are none left to breed. Because of this, there are fewer and fewer fish in the sea. Many countries now have laws to stop too many fish from being caught.

These traditional fishing nets catch larger fish. Smaller fish can escape, grow up and breed.

Fish farms

Many fish are farmed in ponds, or in cages in the sea. About one-fifth of the fish we eat comes from farms. But badly-run fish farms can harm the environment.

Some fish are grown specially in big nets or cages called fish farms. These are often near the coast or in rivers.

Eco Thought
The United Nations says that 75 per cent of the fishing grounds in the world now have too few fish in them.

TO THE SHOPS

It takes a lot of work to get food from farms to shops. Machines do a lot of this work, so the food gets to the shops as fast as possible.

Harvesting

Farmers use machines to harvest wheat. These cut down the wheat plants and thresh it. This means separating the grain from the rest of the plant. Most wheat is harvested this way. Other crops, like tomatoes, lettuces and peas, can be harvested with machines.

Journey to the shops

Fruit and vegetables go from farms to **packing stations**. People there pack them into boxes, and then the boxes are taken to the shops. Animals are killed for their meat, and this is kept cold until it goes to the shops.

These apples are being sorted and packed.

Across the world

Some food is sent from one continent to another, by air, sea or road. It has to be stored carefully, to protect it from pests. Many kinds of food have to travel in refrigerated (cool) containers, so they stay fresh. This is expensive. It is also bad for the environment, as lorries and aircraft give out **greenhouse gases.**

These boxes of broccoli are stored in a special warehouse, where they will be kept cool.

Eco Thought
A machine can harvest a hectare of rice in 2.5 hours. It would take 300 people to do it by hand.

THE FOOD INDUSTRY – How food gets from farms to supermarkets

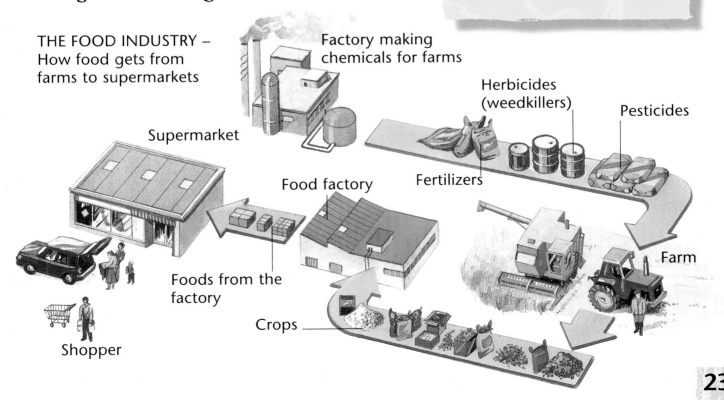

Factory making chemicals for farms

Herbicides (weedkillers)

Pesticides

Supermarket

Food factory

Fertilizers

Farm

Foods from the factory

Crops

Shopper

SAFE FOOD

We all want to be sure that our food is safe. We want to know what happens in the factories that prepare food.

On the Ground
Always wash fruit and vegetables. They may have fertilizer or other chemicals on them.

Clean and safe

Inspectors in food factories and supermarkets check that food is safe to eat. It is important to keep machines clean if they are used to prepare food. Dirty machines may have bacteria (tiny living things) on them. Some of these cause diseases, such as salmonella. People working with food must wash their hands and wear clean overalls, so they don't spread diseases.

In many countries, people buy food in markets. This is a floating market in Thailand.

24

What was added?

Food that is prepared in factories is called processed food. It often contains substances to colour it, or give it extra flavour. We call these **additives.** There are laws to make sure all additives are safe. You can see what these additives are if you look at the label. You can also see what else is in the food, and how much of it is sugar and fat. The label will also have a date on it, to show how long the food will stay fresh.

An inspector checks some beef.

Eco Thought

BSE is a disease that kills cattle. In humans it is called CJD. Cows from herds that have BSE are all killed, to stop it spreading to humans.

Check the labels

People want to know about the food they buy. The labels on the food tell them if the food is all right for them to eat. Labels also show if the food is vegetarian or organic.

Supermarkets sell food that is properly labelled.

FOOD FOR ALL

In some countries, farmers cannot grow enough food for everyone. In others, they grow a lot of food, but it does not always get to everyone who needs it.

These bananas will go bad before they can be carried to people who need them. They have had to be thrown away.

Wasted food

In some countries, too much food is grown. It is not all used and some is thrown away.

Not enough food

In other countries there is not enough food. People get ill because they do not eat well. This is called **malnutrition**. Sometimes, there are droughts or floods, and crops die. People may have nothing to eat. Food can be sent from countries far away. It is easy to send grain and milk powder, but fruit and vegetables can go bad on long journeys. Sending food long distances is expensive, too. Often, the people who need food the most cannot afford it.

These African farmers are learning new ways to look after the land, so they can grow more food.

These people left home because of a war. They have nowhere to grow food. They need food aid.

Solving the problem

When we send food to people, this is called food aid. It is good to do this in an emergency. But most of the time, it is better to help people grow their own food. Organizations called aid agencies help. They may send money to pay for digging wells, or to buy better tools. They can help to irrigate the land. They can teach farmers ways to keep the soil healthy with manure and compost.

Eco Thought
Hydroponics is a way to grow plants without soil. It can even be used in deserts.

WHAT CAN WE DO?

We can all help people in poorer countries to get enough to eat. We can cut down on waste, care for animals and look after the environment.

Help the environment

We can help the environment by buying organic food, so that there is no need for chemical fertilizers and weedkillers. If we buy free-range foods, we know that animals have had good lives. We can choose food that does not have much packaging, so there is less rubbish. If we buy food that has grown close to where we buy it, less exhaust gas from lorries gets into the air.

Labels show shoppers which foods are organic or free-range.

On the Ground

Some organic farmers sell boxes of food to people living nearby. This saves pollution and transport.

Fair trade

Some companies make sure that the people who grow and pick tea and coffee get fair pay. This is called fair trade. Fair trade means farmers can buy better food and tools for their farms. Look for fair trade labels on food you buy.

This woman is picking tea on a tea plantation in India. People work better if they are getting fair pay.

This is fair trade coffee. It is sold in supermarkets.

Sharing

We can all share what we know about growing food. For example, people in poor countries often know the best ways to grow food on their lands. Different kinds of farming help keep different kinds of plants and animals.

FACT FILE

Working the land

Around 45 per cent of people in the world work on the land. Nearly 60 per cent of people in Africa work on the land, but it is only 5 per cent in the United States.

Big potatoes

Potatoes first grew in South America. They were brought to Europe in the 1500s and were grown in North America in the 1700s. Now potatoes grow in about 125 countries.

New crops

Scientists have made new crops. Triticale is one of these. It is a cross between rye and wheat. It does not get diseases easily, and it grows even in poor soil.

Watering the desert

A lot of the land in Saudi Arabia is dry desert. Farmers need to irrigate the land so that crops will grow. The water comes from holes called boreholes. These are drilled deep into the ground.

Plants and animals

We get most of our food from just 12 kinds of plants and 14 kinds of animals.

Population

There are about 6,400 million people on Earth today. In 1900, there were only 1,600 million.

Websites

www.oxfam.org.uk
www.oneworld.net
www.national geographic.com/kids /index.html

GLOSSARY

Additives Substances that are added to foods to make them keep longer, or for colour.

BSE Bovine Spongiform Encephalopaty – a brain disease that kills cattle. When people get the disease it is called CJD.

Calories The units that measure the energy we get from food.

Cash crops Crops grown to sell.

Compost Rotted plants used as fertilizer.

Drought A time with little or no rain.

Fertilizers Substances that farmers add to the land to help crops grow.

Free-range Animals that live outside and can move about.

Genes Tiny parts in the cells of living things. They affect how the living thing develops.

Genetic engineering Taking genes from one plant or animal and putting it into another.

Greenhouse gases Gases in the air that hold heat and keep the Earth warm. Too many are harmful.

Hydoponics A way of growing plants without using soil.

Insecticides Chemicals that kill insects.

Intensive farming A farm that uses modern methods to get as much from the land as possible.

Irrigate To water crops.

Malnutrition Not getting enough good food. A person who has malnutrition will get weak and ill.

Nutrients Substances that are good for the land, and which help crops grow well.

Organic farms Farms where only natural fertilizers, such as manure and compost, are used. These farms also use natural ways to kill pests and weeds.

Packing stations Places where food is packed.

Pesticides Chemicals that kill harmful creatures, such as some kinds of insects.

Pheromone A chemical that insects make. It makes a scent that attracts other insects of the same kind.

Satellite An object that is sent into space, and which orbits (goes round) the Earth or another planet.

Staple crops A food that is the main thing that people eat.

Subsistence farms Farms that produce only food for the farmer and the farmer's family.

INDEX